FIELD GUIDE TO THE LOST FLOWER
OF CRETE

T0096466

THE HUGH MACLENNAN POETRY SERIES

Editors: Allan Hepburn and Carolyn Smart

Field Guide to the Lost Flower of Crete

ELEONORE SCHÖNMAIER

McGill-Queen's University Press
Montreal & Kingston • London • Chicago

ISBN 978-0-2280-0581-0 (paper)
ISBN 978-0-2280-0776-0 (ePDF)
ISBN 978-0-2280-0777-7 (ePUB)

Legal deposit fourth quarter 2021
Bibliothèque nationale du Québec

Printed in Canada on acid-free paper that is 100% ancient forest free
(100% post-consumer recycled), processed chlorine free

Financé par le gouvernement du Canada   Funded by the Government of Canada   Canadä   Conseil des arts du Canada   Canada Council for the Arts

We acknowledge the support of the Canada Council for the Arts.

Nous remercions le Conseil des arts du Canada de son soutien.

Library and Archives Canada Cataloguing in Publication

Title: Field guide to the lost flower of Crete / Eleonore Schönmaier.

Names: Schönmaier, Eleonore, author.

Series: Hugh MacLennan poetry series.

Description: Series statement: The Hugh MacLennan poetry series |
    Includes bibliographical references.

Identifiers: Canadiana (print) 20210117184 | Canadiana (ebook)
    20210117192 | ISBN 9780228005810 (softcover) |
    ISBN 9780228007760 (PDF) | ISBN 9780228007777 (ePUB)

Subjects: LCGFT: Poetry.

Classification: LCC PS8587.C4585 F54 2021 | DDC C811/.54—dc23

This book was typeset by Marquis Interscript in 9.5/13 Sabon.

For

Bruce

CONTENTS

Orpheus with his lute made trees,
And the mountain tops that freeze,
Bow themselves, when he did sing:
To his music plants and flowers
Ever sprung; as sun and showers
There had made a lasting spring.

Every thing that heard him play,
Even the billows of the sea,
Hung their heads, and then lay by.
In sweet music is such art,
Killing care and grief of heart
Fall asleep, or hearing, die.

William Shakespeare

γδύνεσαι όπως γδύνονται όσοι νογούν τ' αστέρια
και μ' οργιές μεγάλες ανοίγεσαι να κλάψεις ελεύθερα

Odysseus Elytis

Εἴμασταν χαρούμενοι ὅλο τὸ πρωῒ
ἡ ἄβυσσο κλειστὸ πηγάδι

George Seferis

AS THE SAND LINES OUR POCKETS

We walk over two bridges
to reach the island where
a shop window reveals a brass

hourglass and a binnacle with
the compass missing. We
head north to the door marked

Nino and enter to find Panos
playing his new music to the rhythm of
the ironmonger's plodding

donkey, and then he guides
us into the melodies of Georgia
and Armenia. Nino fled

Georgia years ago and in her
bedroom I look into three
round mirrors where she wrote

you look fine. She cooks us
soup and as I hold her blue
bowl I stare out the porthole

and find boats
departing for other
worlds. Late that night

traces of our beauty still line
our faces when stolen
time and sunken

compasses
help us retrace
our route.

ENTWINED

Tree roots are entwined into the walls of
the cave, and on the cliffs lining the gorge
goats stand with their tiny hooves as if

suspended in air. Thyme clings, high
and away from the grazing and scents
the air. The gorge bed is all smooth from

past seasons of swirling water and here in the
narrowest section of the trail you reach your
arms wide touching both rock faces. We're tight

together and in the next bend we find
a fleeing donkey trailing a rope as we head
toward the Libyan Sea on this millennia

old trail of escape. The air changes and
we start to feel the salt breezes. At day's
end we walk down over cresting dunes.

We leave shoes, dusty clothes, and worries
behind on the shore. We enter the
turquoise water and joyfully swim forwards.

Last time you gave
me a jar of seaweed
you gathered and pickled for
me. I rationed it out
slowly. Bliss. Did the green bulbous
strands contain an essential
mineral I was lacking or
was it only the memory of
those days on your island? This
time on my last day we
sit in a cafe eating our
favorite lemon tarts and
you reach into your packsack
and bring out three pomegranates
from the tree in your garden.
I pack them gently among
my summer dresses and
at home I set them on
the glass tabletop
afraid to slice
into them.

FERRY

You send me
the message: "I'm
bringing my sister
on the night ferry
from Athens to
Crete." You travel
only with the clothes
you're wearing. The
waning full moon. An
ambulance meets
the boat. You want
Anthie's last days to
unspool at home. In
the living room she
breathes and you
caress her face, her
hands. Her friends
and lovers seated
on the sofa.

Yesterday
we watched
you walk over to
your aunt's house
stopping to look up
at the tall, tall hibiscus.
You stood a long
time and finally chose
a flower. We thought
it was a gift for
your aunt but
later in the day
in your father's
house we saw
the red of
your flower among
the bed of white
roses.

SHOULDERS

Your family dressed in
black formed a receiving
line at the entrance, but
you in a short-sleeved white

shirt remained at the front
of the church seated beside
your sister, your shoulders
fragile beneath the fabric.

Sun on the ropes
and on the wood of

the boat, and the sky
reflected in my glass

of water as if
it was a petal floating

from a blue
flower and what

is the taste of
blue? Years ago

you told me
your sister's name was

Greek for
flower. On the ninth

day prayers are
held at her

graveside and inside
the cemetery gates

we eat ceremonial
koliva: nuts, wheat

raisins, parsley,
and pomegranate

plus silver
garnishes

which you tell me
are not edible.

VISION

You enter
her camera longing
for her selfies
and all you find
are her
visions of
you.

FULL MOON

In your village we
sit beneath the palm
tree where the invasive

beetle is chewing the
heart out of the tree. You
say, "Tonight, Venus is

a mole beside the mouth of
the full moon." The rain
doesn't sound but

dries before it touches
the ground. African sand
browns the sky. The waitress

serves out shot glasses
of rakomelo and each of us
has one minute to

tell a story of love. The lutist's
mother rang the doorbell and
gave her a handwritten letter.

Her first love shunned
her, but the percussionist
says twenty years later she

found him unhappily
married. The guitarist
dated a doctor who

had a box of human
bones under her
bed. You and I are unwilling

to narrate love. A leaf
from the palm tree floats to
the ground. You say, "All the

trees are dying." You show
us a photo of your lost sister
wielding a white plate

she's about to throw
at you and tonight
she's adrift in our sky.

PARAMETERS OF LOSS

The abandoned
airfield is surrounded by
a high barbed

wire fence but
where it meets the
wall of the building

there's a gap, narrow
enough for a small woman and
a slim man to slip

through and they
do. All that expansiveness
is theirs as they walk and

walk and in the distance is
the former air
traffic control tower

but today the sky is
under no one's control.
They're heading east

with no map. Behind the
next high gate is
a barking dog and

space in the fence
for footholds.
They drop over

to the other
side. On the road
they meet only

a legless man riding a
wheelchair. They walk
this way for years.

WHEELS

After Andrew
departed racing
his motorcycle

into the dusk
Luke and I walked
up and down the

flat stones of
the cemetery or
we visited the dump

(it offered up
solutions to most of
our problems).

We found enough
boards for a ramp
and wheels for a

chair. Luke's mother
could now go
outdoors. Even after

he died Andrew
was a regular
visitor but then he left us

behind, or we
left him behind
or he went ahead.

We had no idea.
We searched the ground
covered with

soiled diapers,
condoms, and
empty tins.

We knew the
basics: the screws
and bolts

had to fit and needed
to be strong enough
to hold the mis-

matched wheels.
Berries started to
ripen on the edges

and we shared them
with the bears or
they shared them

with us. We didn't linger
long. We found
a not-bad sofa for

the workshop. We
found a letter
written yesterday.

We didn't know
how to build ladders
to reach platforms

higher than
ourselves, not yet
though we

suspected
we'd be alone
up there.

As teenagers we spent
the entire night
on the Red Lake

in your cedar
canoe. We heard
the heavy rain come

thrumming across the lake's
upper layers. Thunder
and lightning. We

were soaking wet
but it was summer
and warm and when

we finally reached the far
shore, in the full
darkness we climbed

the greased ladder-rungs
of the old mineshaft
house. At the top

we saw the distant town
lights. The others asleep
in their beds. Near dawn

we floated in the star-still
mirror of your ancestors.
Years later we're served

cake, the table set
with red and white tulips
and we sing happy

birthday for our country
who stole you from
your family. The night

on the lake a lightless
boat roared past and
swept back to check if we

were still afloat. They
spoke with silence and
continued on their way.

TOUCHING

You were driving your mother's
rusted-out car down the
dirt road, when your translator
in his pressed white shirt
started touching

the freckles on your
arm. You gave him a stare
that pushed him
head-first into a deep
silence. At eighteen

you were hoping to find
people living on
the logging road, your plastic bag
full of government questions: Census
Canada. In case

French speakers were hiding
in the bush a translator
was tagging along. He looked
stunned when you found a
one room home with a sawed

off stump as the only
chair. The next day alone on
the same stretch of road
a dog silent and unseen charged out
at you and moments later

you were behind a ragged
curtain taking down your
jeans to assess the
wound, realising too late
that ankle-bunched jeans were

a greater danger than a
dog but the man left you
alone untouched behind his
wall of fabric and you stepped
back into the light and

faced him to say, *I'm
ok*. You didn't pass out until
you were back home
seated at the kitchen
table.

I'm lost and walking
on a street where men
from all over the world
prowl as they watch
women sitting in
red-light windows and
I turn left down an
alley and stand
in front of a bright
shop and two
women crowd up
against me and say,
"It's beautiful isn't it?"
as we look at the hand-
woven fabric hanging
loose on a rod and
I note the position
of my purse and I note
the others on the street
and for the first time
that day I feel unsafe
and then the two women
start talking to me
about God.

THE RAILING

She stands on the balcony of
the baron's house. Young,
wavy black hair, her

hands on the railing, face
lined with fatigue. She's wearing an
apron. When the guests

are seated for dinner she and
the other servants open the
cloak room and try

to guess which coat
belongs to which leader.
The baroness

has a teenager's body and her
coat is easy to pinpoint. The one
modeled after a large tomato

is more mysterious
and causes muted
giggling but finds

its way into the letters
she writes for two
years to a man

before she departs
for Canada to
marry him:

he's a gold
miner. They meet
for the first time

when on a warm
day, her coat draped
over her arm,

she steps
off the
ship.

IN THE NEW

She rings out the mop
and cleans the floor
one more time: raw

scraps of meat
all cleared away. Her
daughters at home

asleep. When they enter
school she starts to learn the
new language they

absorb from their story
books. Slowly her boss
switches her shift into

the day and in the back
room she wraps the
meat. The butcher is

often late or
doesn't show up at all
and then vanishes

completely. She studies
the sketches and
starts up the heavy

roar of the saw: this
is her new job. When
she steps out from

the freezer the immense
northern summer
heat washes over her.

It's her first day of
school, and she's
six years old. The idea

of school is the biggest
excitement in her life.
She lives in the northern

wilderness with ice on
her bedroom walls, and
she wants to enter this space

called warm. The teacher
places her in the C unit:
she's in the row with the

Ojibway kids, she's in
the row with the immigrant
kids, she's in the row

with the kids that have drool
coming out of their mouths.
She's in the false prison

labeled *dumb for life* only
she doesn't know what
the word dumb means.

Her father gives her Anne
Frank's *Diary of a Young
Girl*. A stranger gives her

Harriet the Spy. She can't figure
out what a dumb waiter is
or how Harriet can ride up

and down in one. What she knows
is that Anne kept right on writing
when her dinner plate was heaped

high with servings of fear. What
she knows with certainty is
that she has a song in her head

and she wants to write
it down, only she doesn't have the
words. It only takes a few months

for the Ojibway kids and
the immigrant kids to be
smarter than the teacher:

they now know two or three
languages and the teacher only
has one. The kids with drool

are smarter too: they can do
math in their heads, and if they
can't do math they can do kindness

in their hearts and they can do this
at a fast pace. Years later
she still worries and wonders

about the other C row kids.
Did they also escape
rapidly into the A row?

Did they too find the song
in their heads? Give a stranger
a book. Give a stranger a

poem. When a child tells
you that a dumb waiter is
a speechless person who

has to wait a long time
to emerge, say, Yes,
that's right.

Rain: we pull black
garbage bags over our heads
with a hole for our visions
as we sense our way
through the world's raw
wetness. No one gives us
the names and it's only
years later we find
words for where the
music comes from: white-
throated sparrow.

You point to
birds hopping
over pebbles. You hand me

half an eggshell and
we stare inside:
all empty. On the surface

the cream has speckles
of black, umber and blue-grey
some with tiny flags:

your quarter notes.
The Spanish harpsichordist
calls and you say,

"Not decompose,
compose." *Touch of honey
and hints of fresh*

sea air: the cardboard
cylinder from Bowmore Islay
single malt holds the

penciled half-finished
score. You say, "Whiskey
at the beach is

suicide" (the bottle
emptied years ago).
On the sand under

the tree (that drools
salt water at night)
in the cool of

the shade we
work. Birdsong
tangles the branches

but doesn't tear open
our thoughts. To the west
a high peninsula

in haze tapers to its
feet. Short days ago
in the village nearby

we watched as they
lowered your sister
into the earth.

GARDEN

When I arrive
at the house you
search and search

but the tall bushes
reveal only green
leaves. You want to

show me the
flower, "Did my mother
pick it?" You disappear

and return with apricots
placing half
in my hands

and we enter
the living
room: Anthie

in her coma.
Hour
by hour

the doctor
injects opiates.
He shows you how

to rub lotion
into your sister's
back. You go out

and in and
suddenly say, "Come
with me." It's late

afternoon and the flowers
have opened. You show
me how the bees enter

and how their backs are
brushed with pollen
and you gently touch

between my shoulder
blades. At the bus stop
days later a woman

gestures swim, gestures
walk. She wants to know
why I'm here. Suddenly

she touches the black
in the flower of
my fabric and I nod,

yes. And for the first
time I really see
the design of my dress:

the passion fruit flower
from your
garden.

Day after day we
watched you gently
stroking her
forehead as she lost
her breath. Four years
and still it was too
sudden. "What
happened?"
the harpsichordist says. Tubes
pulled out, gauze
strapped under
her chin and we
must leave. Outside
on two red boards
placed over clay planters
the harpsichordist and I sit. A man
wearing blue
gloves races
down the stairs.
The sheet
over her face.
Her mother
strokes her
body, body,
body. Her unbelievable.
Her unbelievably.
Her unbelievably beautiful
face in
the frame
the candle
the

Overlooking the sea
we breakfast on
the hotel terrace.

A tourist comes
up to our table
and says you look

like George Clooney
and you say, "I take it as
a compliment." You're

thirty-five but
your beard has turned
white in the past

year. In India
where you traveled with
your sister for

what you both hoped
was a healing
journey, you found

an enormous
spider in your hot
room. You covered it

with a glass and called
for your sister
to help, but you

never once thought
of killing the spider.
In the funeral procession

we walked on the street
with you and your mother
arm in arm behind

the hearse. Your
sister's friend wore
his T-shirt, *Where*

is the outrage.
People on the
cafe terraces

stood up as we
passed by.
After breakfast

your sister's friend,
the hotel owner,
suggests we go

into the garden
where you tell
me the cacti

with large yellow
edged leaves are
called immortals:

they live a long
life with flowers
growing tall as trees.

While you stand
on the upper

balcony, a red
petal flies

by at eye
level.

We eat lunch on
the balcony with
your parents.
You point out
the apricot trees
resistant to winter
winds. You want to plant
cherry and lemon
trees for the
scent but your father
feels they will
not be sturdy
enough. We eat fish,
potatoes, greens, and
you tell me to
toss the lemon
seeds over
the railing into
the garden
and I do.

TURQUOISE

You're ironing
your turquoise shirt:
swimming in the

warm clear water.
When I enter the
bedroom it's dark

and I hear the iron
giving off steam.
I know you're now

in the kitchen,
the iron turned
off, but the steam

puffs on like an
exhalation until
suddenly it stops.

ISLAND

We row
there together,
we row with

you. The winds
are fierce, the
rain comes

at us sideways.
Our hands
blister on the

wooden oars.
She's there
alone on the

island, your
sister who
went ahead.

The dory pitches
forward. Water
washes over

the sides,
the cliffs are
high. We glimpse

your sister
on the shore.
She waves.

We pull hard on
the oars. We'll
stay a while but

we'll bring you
back. The oars
blister our

hands. We'll
bring you
back.

ROWS

and rows of
hand painted

doorknobs but
no doors.

The man
makes his escape
through the back
door and out there
is nothing but

bush. He's labeled
violent and the staff
let him go. The young
nurse calculates
risks inside her own

head and goes out
after him. By the
time the police arrive
to fetch him back
she knows the wild

will have swallowed
him whole. The man
says, "You're not
my wife." She says,
"No, I'm not," and

they talk to each other
until he feels it's safe
to come back in
and when the two
tall police officers

finally arrive they wear
a *what the fuck* look
on their faces when
they see a young
woman wearing a pink

uniform and a fragile
Alzheimer's patient in
hospital pyjamas sitting
together on the edge
of the bed.

i'm in the bus which is really just an old car
and it's night and pouring rain and i'm
thirteen and the car is jammed with
bodies and we're about to head
down the long dirt road out to
my settlement and the driver
shouts, don't let the drunk
indian in, shouts to close
the door and i slam the
door shut and blood
runs down the
window and a man is out there alone in the
night with a smashed hand but we all
drive off into the dark and i slammed
the door shut on a man's hand and
we drove off into the night
and you tell me how you
held a little girl's hand
and you tell me how she was your first
indigenous friend and i'm not saying
it's not true but if this was the only
truth we would not have the
stories we have
where the drunk man-next-door has a
smashed hand (and i too would have
a bottle in my pocket if i lived in
steady fear) blood running
down the window and there
is a man alone in the night

left to walk to the places
he needs to go when
walking is too far
for any man to
have to go
in all that
cold

a storm
hindering
our vision;

a way of
thinking where
white is the only
colour the viewer
wishes to record;

an antiquated
form of
covering up
errors and facts
dating back to
the era of
typewriters;

officially against
the law to
use whiteout
on government or
legal documents
therefore in officialdom
one uses a
shredder;

families use
clotted white
notes of
silence;

in scores only
the musical
staff remains: an
absence of
celebratory music.

In the
blizzard's epicentre
she finds her skis

and briskly
glides over the
tops of drifts

her thoughts
buried in
whiteness

equal to the span
of her life. She feels
her way back

home into
another night of
high winds. She phones

friends who
arrive to shovel
metres of

snow into
tidy heaps.
Her stranded

lover finally
returns and
marvels at the

clear path where
Venus hangs brightly
above the deck.

will perform in the field across
from my tante's home.
The night of the concert

one of the thirty thousand
visiting fans gives her
his tram seat. Wedged

between the tattooed
men she smiles
out at me. Her body is

full of cancer, she
weighs forty-four-and-a-half
kilograms, but she wishes

to ride the tram home
alone. The following day she
drives us up a mountain, tight

hairpin curve after
tight curve with the
unrailed deep chasm

drop-off to our
right. She wishes
to show us her chosen

burial site: tree
three hundred and
five in the village

forest. We look
down into the valley and
she tells me when she

was thirty her
boyfriend arrived
at her door Friday after

work and said, "We're leaving
at five in the morning to go up
Mont Blanc." She packed

a can of peaches and
they drove to France to scale
the mountain on skis

with two other men.
She recalls the dawn
over the glacier. Arriving

home at six Monday
morning, her feet
were so bloody, the socks

stuck to her skin.
"I showered, changed, and
cycled off to work."

HARNESS

In the Yukon
Ilona in minus forty
degrees is racing

a five hundred
kilometer stretch
on skis alone in

wolf country. She's
the only woman
and her pulk is fully

loaded and harnessed
to her hips.
Somewhere beyond

the shoreline of
Dog Grave Lake her
hallucinations

begin to take
hold. She hears
yelling and realizes

it's her
own voice
and remembers

Lake Laberge
isn't far away. Brief
years ago when she

was a child her teacher
told her about
"The Cremation

of Sam McGee" on
that shore. Ilona
is a small black

dot on white
we track night
after night, day after

day. At Pelly Crossing
huskies and
volunteers curl

up together on
the sofa and
wait. On the seventh

day Ilona
comes in second
and the Italian in

third place loses
both feet and
one hand to

the race and says
he'd do it all
over again.

GOLD

Our fathers worked together under-
ground while you on the surface
gracefully chiselled the ice
the only boy figure skater

in town. Bullies taunted
you with their hockey
sticks. All of us children
of goldminers, and you

decorated with multiple
metals now win gold: Olympic.
Girl in your hands, the first time
you threw her she landed

perfectly. Scared of
heights she trusts you to
twirl her above your head.
Soulmates. Your hidden self

shared with the world. Fear
is a sound in the inner
ear but has no refuge
there.

1   Dynamite Cases

Her two daughters are perched beside her on the wooden
steps of her childhood home. She tells them how years
ago when the gold mine was starting up, her father built
the house from core boxes and the hexagonal covers
of dynamite cases. Sawdust for insulation. She doesn't
say shack.

2   Seedling

Her father works silently in his yard. He cuts an *L* with
his shovel and at the apex, gently nudges in a jack-pine
seedling. His daughter has her own ideas about the earth
and she places the call he asked her not to make, "Yes,
a leaking rust-red tank in the neighbour's yard, the spill
covers the gravel road and seeps into my father's
vegetable garden."

3   Dusk

The daughter knows the neighbour pummelled his older
brother to near death and threatened to run down her
cycling father. In the brief crimson of dusk, when her
children watch arctic terns swoop like whipped blades
she no longer knows which hovers more steadfastly:
beauty or danger.

4   Bird-air

Alone at night with her children, her father's kitchen
table butted to the door, she feels not regret but layers
of stacked fear pushing into her body. Lying awake she
unfolds, like old letters, the knowledge that her father
esteems all women as strong protectors: garden-soil,
bird-air, child-breath.

5   Bones

She rubs the lines in her left palm. Earlier in the day the
neighbour stepped close to her and the only sentence she'll
repeat to her children: "Go back to where you came from –"
A cave, an open fire, a handful of bones. Trying to put
herself to sleep, she reads about fossilized netting: hints
of women and children gathering birds in field-wide nets.

LABYRINTHITIS

Send me a
ball of red

wool held in the
beak of a

bluebird and
I will find

my way back out
to the auricle

framing the sounds
of the sky.

When the nerve for
balance in her right
inner ear ceases to

function the voyage
from bed to bathroom
requires new navigation

skills, her body leaning
left as she gropes for
the wall on the right

and sometimes
she can't get that far.
Her bed

becomes a ship at
sea and her ex-sailor holds
her hair back as she

vomits into the white
bowl. In the midst
of the five vertigo-months

Valentijn drops maps into
her mailbox and she begins
to visualize her way

back out into the world as
she reads his note about
the inner heart of the nearby

nature reserve emptied
of people and filled
with stillness. Her physio-

therapist trains her by
pitching two-kilogram balls
at her while she balances

on one foot. Months
later she holds the
map where the red

arrow marks the entrance
but on the actual trail
there are no signs.

She finds the opening
in the fence and enters the songs
of skylarks and among

the blossoms of the
hawthorn bushes are six wild
white horses.

As you walk into
the park a single
bee enters

the mouths
of the jewel
weed in this last

light of dusk
and you hear a white
horse walking

over two
white bridges
and in the playground

you swing higher and
higher while a
tawny owl

lands in
the sand
at your feet.

Each day the horses
acquire more wounds.
We've had no
rain for many weeks

and they fight over the
yellowing grass. Bees
fly erratically and bump
into our faces, first

mine and then yours.
All their nectar has dried
up. Seed pods litter the
ground as if it was autumn

but it's midsummer. No
wind. Heat. The only sweetness
left is the cool moisture
of your lips.

CIRCULAR

Usually the great blue heron wades
in the water looking
down, but today she's on the shore

gazing skywards as she walks a perfect
circle. You and I have never worn
our wedding bands. On a side

trail we used to sit
on our favorite white bench
until the boards rotted and one

day the bench was no longer
there; on the same hummock
the great storm tore the trees

down. At dusk
I lead you back there
and we find a circular bench

built around the
trunk of a freshly planted
poplar tree. We rest holding

hands in the dwindling
light watching the heron standing
· still waiting for the

large fish we saw
last week swimming
in this pond.

FISH CAMP

Her boss picks her
up at six on
Saturdays. His

station wagon is
wide enough that if she
squirms against the passenger

door his hand
barely touches her
thigh. Along the dirt

road dewy spiderwebs
shine in the early
morning light as he

asks if she has
a boyfriend and she lies
and says, Yes. At the lakeside

camp she watches
him swat the ass of the
other sixteen-year-old

girl. The men board
boats to go fishing
while she changes

the stained
sheets, pissed in
from too much

beer the night
before. That evening
parked in front of

her rental home
the dollar bills are
warm in her

jean pocket,
plastic wrapped
walleyes in her lap.

DIVING

Infotech + Biotech =

The big fish are
not swallowing us whole.
They're diving

deep into our
small inner
selves but

they're not lying still
on the cutting
board of who

we think we are
waiting
to feed us, no, they're swimming

through and the self we
thought we possess
the self we thought

we are is no
longer
the self.

MULTITUDE

Silver-blue fish like a living curtain
brush in their multitude against
her. Crested terns dive

into the sea. Her lover waits on shore
for the coming of their twelve thousandth
night. He wraps her dragonfly sarong

around her dripping cool skin. When they walk barefoot
in the sand a herd of ten horses and riders canter
through the swash marks: the tiny shells

and debris. They climb the steep stairs, holding on
to the metal railing, and at the top the old
thin man who stands there at sunset each day

stands there again. Switching on their bicycle lights
they cycle down the hill at top speed holding
hands even around the most precarious corners.

My tante clutches her purse
close to her body as we
watch Nino and Enrico play

the two piano rendition of
Liszt's *Les Préludes* and
at dinner she tells us

when she was a child
Joseph Goebbels broadcast
Liszt's music before

"the news full of lies."
I've sent her spiraling
into our cold past.

In our future we
watch Heiner Goebbels's
Stifters Dinge: five

piano keyboards play
without musicians
as rain falls into

three pools. Mist rises
in front of the skeletal
outlines of trees.

Industrial objects hiss,
squeak, clink, whirr.
When we cycle

home through the silent
forest my tante
talks about a woman

who could not sleep
when she was a child
because of the

nightingales singing.
"Can you imagine
a time when there

was so much song
in the air it would
distress you?"

BRANCHES

Usually when you visit
you sleep in the Drachen-

gäßchen, but this time
you overnight in the alley

house behind my home
with the high window

overlooking my garden.
In rain and wind we climb

the mountain and we talk
about Heidegger's

Holzwege but today we
don't stumble into

his dead ends. At the cold
peak we recline on a bench with

a view into the valley and
we share green tea from

my Thermos: in which year
did we start drinking out of

the same warm cup? A long
time ago you picked up

a pen and the history you wrote
was the future where

we would enter
the music, note

by note. Today we whistle
with the songbirds but

the past never leaves us alone
especially when it was lived

before we were born.
Your tante as a child

of war fled down the
paths that crisscross

this forest. The houses
on the Drachengäßchen

are now under
demolition but

their ghosts live on
and in your sleep they

try to grab you. Today
I guide us down

the dangerous side
path, the one leading to

full safety, and we
remember how

Heidegger refused to find
a safe route for

his friends in need
when he traced out his

thoughts. At the trail's
branch I hold out

my bottle of water and
we both drink deeply.

In the Nova
Scotian forest
she rushes
out into
the dark
holding a
closed book
that opens into
a fan of light,
and she watches
the leaves of
the yellow
birch tree,
the white birch
tree, and her lover in
the shower behind
frosted glass
while deer
rustle among
the bushes
and she
re-enters just
in time to
hand him
his towel.

TOUCHSTONE

Your ex-lover gave you my
number and you called
and said, "You don't know

me," but your name
lodged years ago in
my mind. I met you at

the bus station and I said,
"I had no idea what
you look like," but you saw

me right away in my red
dress. In those next
days before or after

her last breath
you and I wandered aimlessly
down a hot abandoned

coastal street carrying only
our mobiles. We had left everything
else behind. I found

then a white beach pebble
and held it for hours.
I still search in

my memory for how
and when I lost it.
Later in our

home city I reach into
my coat pocket and
say, "Oh," and you

say, "The pebble,"
but it's a chocolate
Easter egg and

we stare as if I'd pulled
a maggoty rabbit
out of a hat.

REMEMBER

the world before you
held a glowing
screen in your hand to

shield you from
the beauty of the
dragonflies pairing above

the apple tree, of the
comet falling across
the diagonal of

the southwest,
of the wild rabbit
with long ears

that twitch and listen,
of the hummingbird
visiting your

lover in his blue-green
hammock beneath
the maple trees.

In India
while caring for
your sister you fell
in love with
the taste of barley.
A year later during
the full hunger moon
the comet Mrkos
reaches its closest
path to Earth
on the night of
your world
premiere of *Kāma*:
flute, clarinet,
cello, trumpet, viola,
and the comet
visible in
the constellation
Hercules just before
sunrise –

SAND

We were given
tapered candles
to light and
we placed them
in circles of sand
and at the end we
watched a woman
snuff them out
and store them
in a metal bin.

We had met only two days
before and were now departing

on the same flight. On the
airport floor we open

our suitcases moving your
belongings into mine to

balance the weight. You
say, "You're not supposed

to let strangers put
things into your luggage"

and we laugh surrounded
by tourists. Waiting for

takeoff we talk nonstop
as if we've known each

other all our lives. This
wasn't a journey

we'd planned. Back
home you'll give me

funeral music as
a gift saying, "I looked on

my shelf and it could
only be this."

GLYPHS

We've lost
many ancient
stories. The clay

disk of Phaistos
on Crete still hides
its spiral

tale. To walk in
the cypress forest is
to contemplate the disk and

its glyphs: the
heads and hands,
birds, fish,

and flowers. To want
all people to
plant the garden where

the dead survive in tree
spirals on top of
their graves.

WAITING

We walk
along streets littered
with leaves from

last night when
the winds swayed the
trees and as we stroll

through their love
letters too lost in
our own languages to

read the veins and
stems, we cross
the red bridge to enter

the forest where
I lead you to the
oldest tree

and there under
its branches
you talk about

your refugee friend who
waiting five years to know
whether he could stay

started his new life with
his girlfriend and the birth
of their child only to

be judged and
told, you should
have waited

and today alone
he has to return
to the Congo

and his
other world
terrors.

BOTTLING

The city loves its Congo
bananas, but which one
of over one thousand

varieties is the right
flavour for a new liqueur?
In the Leuven

labs and greenhouses
the banana genes
are preserved

so when illness strikes
the fruit will survive.
The plant geneticist

and the brewer talk
about *musa* mixed
with rum and honey.

What did we lose
forever when
the conquerors

drank liquor
from Congolese
skulls? The bottles

stand empty
through millennia
waiting to preserve

the formula
for what the heart
feels.

Building materials this
week are torn, broken,
mismeasured, mis-

numbered, or just
plain late. Repeatedly
I stand in front of

shops where I fall into
the frame of the hours
posted but the doors

are locked, lights on
dim. Yet suddenly here's
a luminous window and

when I push the door
gently I find an opening,
find chairs so

comfortable I might
have to take them home
for when I finally sit

evenings in the new
spaces. The upholsterer
tells me he's from

Iran. I say, Canada.
He says something
about a car

while I'm picturing
how to strap
his chairs onto

my bike carrier.
We gesture and
speak an alternative

language foreign to
both of us. He'll put new
fabric on the old

frames. We'll sit
together between
worlds, those

we've lost and
those we're
creating.

QUINZHEE

The walls are insulated with
sawdust and it's so cold you
can almost see your breath
as you sit on the wooden bench

in front of the black
and white keys. You intuit
that heat
is a state of motion

whose measure
is temperature: your fingers
feel too slow and frozen
to thaw the correct pitch

into music. You want to run
quickly outdoors through
the drifts, or crawl into
the quinzhee that your father

created out of a pile of snow.
Mostly you burrow into the whole
notes stored inside your mind
until decades later in a southern

home your fingers
find the new music
you've waited for
all these years.

I drop in
through the skylight
and you say, "I hope
you didn't break too
many roof tiles." I'm
surprised by your lack
of surprise, but of course
you've been expecting me to
enter via the sky ever since
I told you about my nocturnal
activities. We stand now
together on your bathroom
floor neither of us knowing
what to do. You'd been
hanging your hiking
shorts on the drying
rack beneath the
windows and I was
placed in danger by
all that metal wire. The
bedroom door is ajar
across the hall. I
say, "Shall we play
Schubert together? I've
only heard you from
out on the street. We
could do the four
hands piece you've
been practising" and
we do so as naturally
as if this wasn't
our first time.

We walk upstairs
and the world falls
away from us. In

the morning when
we descend we're
shocked to find the

doors and windows
all wide open. We'd
forgotten everything

during the night when
the heavy rain entered.
My electric

keyboard flooded with
water but we know
exactly what to do.

We unplug and lay the keys
upside-down on the
sofa and all is saved

especially the lightness
of how I floated
on top of you.

OUTSTRETCHED ARMS

I walk to the village
fountain, carrying empty
bottles. I pass the yard

with the skull and
crossbones flag propped up by
concrete bricks, the high

wire mesh fence. Symbol of
a stick person: the outstretched
arms joined by a half circle, painted on

many walls to keep
homes safe from bad spells or
storms. Yesterday single drops

fell from the sky and an old man
pointed and said *mojar*.
I remain dry and dusty. I walk on

marble, bend low over
the spout, cup my hands,
and drink slowly.

I wash my face. A man
removes his shirt. He touches
the water.

Shell of a snail on the cracked
desert earth: spiral
of auburn and blue opening
into a small tuba's mouth.
Children want to stretch
their tongues out. Instead they walk
in beige dust clouds and poke sticks
into the earth as it splits
away from itself. A few raindrops
and the children will speak
the word for green.

If the winds do not blow too strong –

Northern mining children kick
the soccer ball and it tumbles
over the grey-soil fissures: the cyanide
field. They find abandoned shells
the red casings of bullets,
a blue water pistol, a red truck with its black
wheels crushed, and no blade
of grass. When the rain comes green
is the paint-by-number colour
outside the playground.

A dog with nose to
the ground reads the

scent, the many different
story lines all

at once: the dog
highways. At 4:00 a.m.

the dogs speak
to each other. With

nine languages in
the house, the musicians

are still not multilingual
enough. One large black

dog panting, runs past
the lower rooms or

so the cellist says. She hears
chewing under the palm tree.

The percussionist rises
to check for human

intruders. Only the
pianist, whom dogs

usually attack, sleeps through
the night. As though the dogs

were the first to know,
the rain begins

to fall in the desert
briefly.

On the edge of the Sambro
ballfield the Johnny
on the Spot is

in a metal cage. Valuable
things get stolen
here, but I want to roll

a grand onto the field: it seems
like the perfect stage for
4'33" with the score

augmented by the American
Redstarts and the sound of
my breathing. I pace

the rhythm and add some
rubato. The tall man standing
beside his truck squints, and

I know he's thinking, Why are
you crouched as if there's a chair
and why are your hands in midair?

I say, Can't you see the grand?
Don't you hear the Cage? I count
the quavers of his confusion. *If*

*you need help I'm right
here,* he says, and hands me
his card. Al Vogeler. Electrician.

I've been having problems with
my keyboard, I say. *My brother
works with keys if you're locked*

*out or that kind of thing. He
can get you back in.* I'm locked
out of my field, I say. He

says, *This field is wide
open. This field is all
yours,* and I start to feel

he's rewiring the hope back
into my brain. The others
at the competition stole first,

second, and third. But Al's right,
I can still step back in
from the outfield. I say,

Oh, and do you have a
key to that cage? It's kind
of urgent.

BEETHOVEN AND THE DOORBELLS

I grab my coat, the dog
heels and the door closes
behind me. I'm on the street

with no keys, no wallet, no
phone. After walking the dog
I wanted to catch the bus into

the city where I'm the soloist
in Beethoven's fourth piano
concerto. It's not my dog,

not my home, and I simply
can't be late. I begin
ringing the doorbells of all

the neighbours. It's the age of
robots and drones but
a woman knows how to

use a coat hanger and
within twenty minutes I'm back
in. I've spent years

alone in my room
preparing for the
moment when I'd be

asked to perform on this
stage: the opening
notes of the piano as

the orchestra is
silent. Beethoven wrote
the strings' gruff phrase as if

it's a funeral march and
the piano's fragile reply.
The orchestra interrupts

the piano and then starts to
soften through another
sequence, and finally

the piano finds its voice
and each day is my own
improvised cadenza.

Wolfert's hair is brushed
straight back at the sides
and he looks as if he's facing

into a gale-force wind as he sits
at the keyboard surrounded by
string quartet and percussion.

His improv and score
evokes our ruin
and resilience. En route

to the concert in a
back alley I saw
an abandoned high

chair with the seat
overlaid by a large
fallen leaf. How

do children survive
war? Through
thin walls I heard

my parents screaming
at night in their sleep
reliving over and

over their youth.
My mother
saw a paratrooper

walk down the street
with a stake jutting
out of his leg and she

visited her mother
in prison: the open
wounds on her

limbs. Wolfert
nods and the drumming
begins.

APPLAUSE

only the rhododendrons   remain green, and the blades
         of grass   buried beneath   the dead leaves

on the white bench in the melting
              hail is a   glove someone   left behind

just outside the park the loud-   clang white-metal gate of   the military
              compound opens to   let in the   squatters

they begin their   percussion as if   Wolfert was
              whispering in their ears

the precipitation is now   pure
                                             rain
the washed away snow and
                   hail is not a blank
                          slate where we can   begin again

we've grown unaccustomed to
              endings as if we've also
                   forgotten the meaning of   applause

INSTRUMENT OF TROUBLED DREAMS

Chiara enters the church,
walks to the High Choir
and sits down at

the Instrument of
Troubled Dreams and begins
to play. It's exactly three

weeks since she read
Florestan's last message—
the first key brings

forth a woman's
voice: "she doused
her light and stood

silently in
the shadows listening
intently." Keys

marked *wind gusts*,
raven – the whoosh
of wings filling the

entire church. *Rain,
thunder,* and *water
drips*. Her mind empties

and fills – the church is a
time machine – *helicopter*
and *guns,* past wars

and future floods. *Stairs
creaking, boots on roof,* more
rain, and *Sweelinck* plays

his organ. For these past weeks
when she's been unable to
sleep, Sweelinck's music

in her bedroom has saved her
when Florestan crashed
into her dreams. All

the centuries folded into
one. The eeriness of
his *Carnival.* Where is

he now? She has
no idea. They've lost
each other in too many

words and too many silences.
She closes her eyes but
can no longer find

his eyes and in the inner
darkness she seeks the keys –
main sail, breathing –

The blue wooden chair
inside the metal cage
is large enough for a human-size sonata
to rest there deep

in thought. A man in a blue sweater looks
in and what is he thinking
as he stands beside the woman
wearing a red

scarf? He reads the hand-
writing pinned to the cage
and recognizes the baroque
composer. Together they walk the corridors

of the cloister, the walled
courtyard. They leave behind
the sonata breathing softly,
sitting still.

You step out
of your sheepskin
slippers and I step

into your warmth
your feet larger
than my own, granting

new ways for our
familiar expansiveness.
You serve spanakopita,

sweet wine and
returning to our
boots we climb

the mountain at
dusk. Leaves wet
and bronzy on

the ground as our
conversation roams
through all we need

to roam: the sonata
you wrote for your brother
and how by chance

your music came to life
in my ancestral landscape.
Earlier with my tante

I watched five swans
take flight from the lake
swooping away and circling

back and suddenly
they were right overhead
all that wingspan

blue-sky motion and all over in
brief moments. You and I
descend in the dark

vineyards in silhouette, river
glistening until we're back
under city lights

in your high ceilinged
room where you play
Shostakovich for me.

You speak softly
about how you found
the score as a child

your face lit by one
lamp and there's briefly
a true-depth calmness

before I again see
the pallor of
your grieving.

LAKE

The sun needs to
reaffirm her luminous
beauty and in doing so

blinds us. The moon
wishes to race
her chariot

and leaves us
stranded in her dust
but still sun and

moon guide us
day or night on the path
through the forest.

I stretch my arms
in the water and the stars
send their light

that always and
always arrives
too late here

at the edge
where your sister
found you.

CHOCOLATIER

In the Trojan Horse
bookstore and cafe
we read Cicero

who reminds us
old age will be the
best time of

life. We drink
hot chocolate and
look out at the

square full of
vibrant university
students. It feels as if

we've been smuggled
inside another
world. Too many

young friends have
died recently. As we step
outside a time-worn

tugboat floats
down the canal.
Even boats grow

old in Ghent,
given tender care. In
the chocolate store

I buy the flavour
labelled *old books:*
"based on the scent

of the university
library in Bologna."
The chocolatier is a

former archeologist
who has left behind
the unburying of

the past to create
our present. But
what is each day if

not layers and
layers of collective
memory? The

chocolate is a mini
gold-brushed
brick where the edges

crumble and melt on
our tongues: hazelnut,
salt, tobacco, and myrrh.

Do you remember the
room in Ghent full of
too many angels? I found

a short skirt (perfect
for cycling) in the
second-hand shop

where the woman
told me I had gorgeous
breasts. The wings

in the room were
golden and white but
(thankfully!) there was no

motion, no flight. Only
you and me forgetting
to be still in that overly

large bed so that we
were both shocked and
amazed when their harp

strings and feathers
floated down
upon us.

the guests who   sleep
in her house come   and
go. they never find   her

there but they   feel
her morning sunlight, her   red
door, her pomegranate   tree

her white table, her   laughter
her turquoise chair, her   loves
her sea, her blue-white   dress

her Panama hat, the one   she
gave her brother as a   gift
look, it rests over   there

just there   on
the pillow of   the
double   bed

ACKNOWLEDGMENTS

"it didn't happen here" won the 2019 National Broadsheet Contest from the League of Canadian Poets, judged by D.A. Lockhart.

"Johnny on the Spot" received an honourable mention in the Great Blue Heron Poetry Contest from the *Antigonish Review*, judged by Sue Goyette.

Michalis Paraskakis based his music-theater multimedia work *Field Guide* on selected poems (for one piano, two pianists, electronics, and video).

With thanks to the following publications where some of the poems in *Field Guide to the Lost Flower of Crete* were published (often in earlier versions and sometimes under alternative titles):

"Entwined" in *Wild Gods: The Ecstatic in Contemporary Poetry and Prose* (New Rivers Press, United States)

"Afloat" in *Arc Poetry Magazine* (in a special "Oh, Canada" edition edited by Armand Garnet Ruffo)

"In the New" in *White Wall Review*

"The Dumb Waiter" in *The Best Canadian Poetry Blog* (Tightrope Books)

"Compose" in *Arc Poetry Magazine*

"Lemon Tree" in *Stand Magazine* (United Kingdom)

"Pink" in *Prairie Fire*

"'it didn't happen here" in the League of Canadian Poets'
Poem in Your Pocket Day Brochure, as a broadsheet
created by artist Briar Craig, as a postcard designed
by Megan Fildes, and online as part of the Poetry
Pause for World Poetry Day on March 21, 2019

"Whiteout" in *The Antigonish Review*

"Inner" in *Wild Gods: The Ecstatic in Contemporary
Poetry and Prose* (New Rivers Press, United States)

"Fish Camp" in *Fireweed*

"Outstretched Arms" in *Grain*

"Tongues" in *Grain*

"So Much Remains Invisible" in *Grain*

"Johnny on the Spot" in *The Antigonish Review*

"Outside the Lamplight Circle" in *Voicing Suicide*
(Ekstasis Editions)

"Lake" in *Voicing Suicide* (Ekstasis Editions)

Out of admiration for their courage, I wish to thank the
women in my family for their inspiration. Thank you also
to Frederic Rzewski for answering my questions about
social class, love and joy, and Henriëtte for finding the
Shakespeare epigraph. Gracias Jorge por encontrarme
en el laberinto. Ευχαριστώ τον Πάνο, έναν υπέροχο δάσκαλο
στη μουσική και στη ζωή. Ευχαριστώ τον Μιχάλη, που βρήκε
τις σωστές λέξεις με τον κατάλληλο τρόπο, και για τόσα άλλα.

"Afloat" is for Roy.

NOTES

The William Shakespeare epigraph is from *King Henry the Eighth*, Act III, Scene I.

The Odysseus Elytis epigraph is from "Ο Νεφεληγερέτης," translated as "The Cloudgatherer," *Odysseus Elytis: Selected Poems*, trans. John Stathatos and Nanos Valaoritis (New York: Penguin Books, 1981). The epigraph is translated as: *you undress as those who pay attention to the stars undress/and with wide strokes you swim out in order to weep freely.*

The George Seferis epigraph is from "Διάλειμμα Χαράς," translated as "Interlude of Joy," *George Seferis: Collected Poems*, trans. Edmund Keeley and Philip Sherrard (Princeton, NJ: Princeton University Press, 1981). The epigraph is translated as: *The whole morning long we were full of joy; /the abyss a closed well.*

AS THE SAND LINES OUR POCKETS: *There once was a donkey* (2016) for tape and piano written and performed by Greek composer and pianist Panos Gklistis (1985).

HARNESS: Ilona Gyapay (1992) is a Canadian extreme athlete who was born and raised in the Northwest Territories. She was both the youngest and the only woman to compete in the 482 kilometre stretch of the Yukon Arctic Ultra in 2018, which was the coldest year in the event's history with temperatures dropping as low as -55°C. She outlasted some of the top male adventure racers in the world. "The Cremation of Sam McGee" is a poem by Robert Service (1874–1958). In his poem Robert Service changed the name of Lake Laberge to Lake Lebarge to create the rhyme with marge.

GOLD: Eric Radford (1985) is a Canadian figure skater and the first openly gay man to win Winter Olympics gold. Together with his partner Meagan Duhamel (1985) they were 2018 Olympic gold medallists in the team event, 2014 Olympic silver medallists in the team event, and 2018 Olympic bronze medallists in the pairs event.

SLEEPLESS: Georgian Nino Gvetadze (1981) and Italian Enrico Pace (1967) are concert pianists. Heiner Goebbels (1952) is a German composer and director. His *Stifters Dinge* (2007) is a play with no actors, a composition for five pianos with no pianists. Austrian writer Adalbert Stifter (1805–1868) focused his attention on non-human forces, natural phenomena, and "things" we don't really know how to name and explain.

BRANCHES: *Holzwege* literally means dead-end logging roads and figuratively means to take the wrong path. It is also the title of one of Heidegger's books. Martin Heidegger (1889–1976) was a German philosopher.

HUNGER: *Kāma* (2016) by Greek composer Michalis Paraskakis (1980) was premiered at the Impuls Festival 2017 performed by Klangforum Wien and Enno Poppe (bass flute, heckelphone, bass/contrabass clarinet, contraforte, tubax, trumpet, horn, trombone, harp, viola, cello, double bass).

JOHNNY ON THE SPOT: John Cage (1912–1992) was an American composer. *4'33"* (1952) is a three-movement composition that instructs the performer not to play their instrument during the entire duration of the piece. Al Vogeler (1973) is a Nova Scotian electrician and former fisherman.

THROUGH THIN WALLS: *Ruins and Remains* (2018) by Dutch composer and pianist Wolfert Brederode (1974) was written to commemorate the end of World War I.

INSTRUMENT OF TROUBLED DREAMS: Created by Canadian installation and sound artists Janet Cardiff (1957) and George Bures Miller (1960), the *Instrument of Troubled Dreams* (2018) is a surround-sound experience. Cardiff and Miller transformed a mellotron by programming each of the seventy-two keys to produce a different sound effect, and the public were invited to come and play. Words in italics are the labels of specific keys. Jan Pieterszoon Sweelinck (1562–1621) was a Dutch composer.

CHOCOLATIER: Nicolas Vanaise (1963) is a Belgium creator of edible art and former Middle East archeologist. Bologna University was founded in 1088.

The author's webpage can be found at:
https://eleonoreschonmaier.com